BUSINESS INSIGHTS

"Building a Healthy Business"

Jerry Walters

Printed in the United States of America

ISBN-13: 978-1546663720

ISBN-10: 154666372X

10 9 8 7 6 5 4 3 2

Empire Publishing

www.empirebookpublishing.com

Contents

BUSINESS INSIGHTS

Passionate Objective

This is the fuel that powers the business - the spark that ignites action - the heart and soul of the business - the source of excitement and enthusiasm - the purpose of going to work every day - a catalyst for fun.

A passionate objective is the crystal clear mental image of the business's purpose that generates the ideas, strategy, action, motivation, enthusiasm, and energy to make that mental image a reality.

Picture in your mind, planning the most wonderful trip you have ever taken. How do you feel? Do you feel happy, excited, and energetic? What does it arouse within you? If you are like me, it creates the motivation and energy to make it happen. I enthusiastically begin to think about how to make the vision of that trip a reality. I begin to plan. I think about how I am going to get there, where I will stay when I arrive, what I will need to take with me, who I will invite to go with me, when will I leave and how long will I be gone, how much money I will need for the trip and where will I get that money. My point is that if I have a passionate objective, a crystal clear mental image that creates excitement and energy I will take action. A passionate objective will stimulate my thought processes. I will plan and execute the plan.

A passionate objective creates focus within an organization. This focus becomes the center of business decisions. Just like in planning a trip, it drives the decisions of the how, what, where, who, and when of accomplishing the objective. It makes the decision-making process more fun and effective when everyone in the organization has a crystal clear image of where the business is going and why it exists.

I recently read a book entitled "Success Built to Last - Creating a Life That Matters." It was published by the Wharton School. A group of very talented people interviewed over 200 other people from around the world in a variety of fields and professions. They interviewed unknown business managers, entrepreneurs, teachers, Olympians, and Nobel laureates, as well as Pulitzer, Grammy, Peabody, Academy Award winners, and the CEO's of large and small organizations. The major criteria as to whom they interviewed was that the person had to have been successful in their respective field for at least 20 years. One of the major themes of the interviews was that successful people have one or more passions and these passions compel them to overcome obstacles, the passions create energy, they have fun, and they have meaning in their lives. I suggest that is what a business must do. A healthy business must have a passionate objective that will ignite action, generate energy, create enthusiasm, and bring focus to decision making.

Brand

Brand is not marketing! Marketing is what you do to promote a product or service. Brand is what sets a business apart from other businesses in the same or similar industries in the minds of clients and prospective clients. Brands can be simple, such as the Nike brand. A brand creates awareness in the mind of the client. A brand is what people remember about a business.

A brand brings home the reality of the old adage "a picture is worth a thousand words." Once a brand is established through various means of promotion, it is a very effective and cost-efficient method of bringing clients and revenue to a business. Think of the leverage a business can get from a recognizable brand. That simple Nike brand sends a multitude of messages to the marketplace. When worn by golfers it sends the message that Nike is a business of golf shoes and apparel. When on a football player it sends the message that Nike is a business of football shoes and apparel. The point is a healthy business must establish an effective brand in the minds of those in their respective marketplace.

However, brands can have difficulties in getting established. The most important aspect of establishing a brand is to choose one and stick with it over time. Again, the purpose is to get it established and recognized in the minds of the people in their marketplace. It has been proven again and again that repetition is the best method of impacting the conscious and subconscious mind of a human being. When my first child was born, I really did not grasp this concept. I was in the fairy tale world of "if I say it once or twice, it should stick." If you have children, you know what I am talking about, right!!!! I am sure you can conjure up images of things like potty training, learning to drink from a glass, or learning to dress themselves. The point is that before their conscious and subconscious mind said "I remember" it took repetition, repetition and more repetition. The same is true with creating a brand. It is repeating the brand visually and/or audibly over and over in the minds of the marketplace. Once the brand is established in their minds, then the leverage of the brand becomes enormous.

There is another very important aspect of a brand, and that is the brand image. Many businesses work for years to create a brand that its customers, marketplace, alliances and employees trust and respect. However, due to changes in culture, business practices, and just plain bad business decisions, the brand loses that trust and respect. Once a brand becomes tainted it becomes very difficult, and expensive, to regain that positive image of the brand. The goal should be to establish and maintain, through ethical business decisions, a well-respected image among customers, the marketplace, alliances, and employees.

The culture of the business is an important aspect of image. The perception and reality of culture impacts many aspects of the business. A culture of trustworthiness, integrity of decisions, focus on the people in the organization, quality products and services, and a pattern of following through on commitments to employees, clients, and alliances. All of these things will impact a client's willingness to buy from the business, a person's desire to work for the business, a supplier's desire to associate with the business, a lender's desire to loan money to the business or an investor's willingness to invest in the business. Whether perceived or real, cultural image will impact all of these.

Another aspect of a well-respected image is the business's environment. Is the environment safe for employees? Is the physical plant clean? Is the employee environment fun, challenging and rewarding? Is the physical location of the business in an area that is viewed as a desirable location?

The point is there are many factors that affect a well-respected image, which in turn affects the brand of the business. A healthy business ensures that the brand is a leverage point for revenue and employee growth.

Value - Added Leadership

Value added leadership is the value that the business owner or owners and the key executives in the business bring to every aspect of the business. Value added leadership is the direct opposite of being the boss. The difference being that value added leaders serve the business while bosses expect the organization to serve them. Let's explore the characteristics of value added leadership.

First, let's address what value added leadership is not. It is not being the boss and does not seek personal credit for the business's successes. Instead, value added leadership lets go of pride and ego to serve the organization and gives away the credit to others. There have been a number of books written about organizations that have had lasting success and, in every case, a critical factor has been that the leadership of the organization let go of ego and humbly served the business. They focused on doing what is in the best interest of the business as a whole and not what would be in their best interests personally, whether that be money or personal recognition.

Value added leadership breathes life into the "passionate objective" of the business. Value added leaders are focused on the passionate objective of the business, each and every day, and consistently seek ways to bring life to the passionate objective among the people within the organization. These leaders are positive and enthusiastic about the business's "passionate objective" and take every opportunity to transfer that passion to others in the organization. They talk about the passionate objective and the benefits of that objective to clients and employees.

Value added leaders accept responsibility and accountability for business decisions and recognition for good decisions is given away to others in the business. For a bad decision they do not point fingers at others; they do not blame the decision on bad luck nor do they make excuses for the decision. They accept accountability and responsibility for the decision, learn from the experience, and then move on.

Value added leaders have a healthy perspective on financial results. They recognize that positive financial results are the life blood of the business, but other considerations, such as the people in the organization, are important as well. These leaders recognize that factors outside the control of the business affect financial results such as national, state, and local economic changes. This is not to say that value added leaders minimize the importance of financial results but they do recognize there are many aspects to being a healthy business, and financial results should be considered as one piece of the business puzzle.

Value added leaders are grounded in reality. They don't hide their head in the sand if things are not going well. They do not rely on the "hope" that things will turn around. Rather they evaluate the business as it is today, create models for future success, and then execute. They objectively assess the capabilities of the people in the organization, accurately measure activity, and track results on a regular basis. I will talk about processes and systems in a few minutes, but one of the qualities of a value added leader is that they have a system of measuring the health of the business. They review the critical numbers of the business on a very regular basis, accept those numbers as they are, and then make decisions based on the reality of the numbers. They assess the true skills and capabilities of their employees and make decisions based on the reality of those skills and capabilities. They base today's decisions on the reality of the business's condition today.

Value added leaders put the right people in the right place. Put another way, they put the right people on the bus. They objectively evaluate the needs of the business, objectively evaluate the skills, abilities, and attitudes of people, and then hire the people that meet the needs of the business. They do not make people decisions based on hiring friends, relatives, referrals, etc., unless the skills, abilities, and attitudes of these people match the needs of the organization. We will talk more about the right people in the right place in a few minutes.

Value added leaders get extraordinary results from ordinary people. Once the right people are in the right place, then value added leaders help them visualize how they can be better than they are today, and then help them make that vision a reality. They create a framework of recognition, inspiration, and education that brings more value to the organization through the employee's growth. Value added leaders recognize small and big successes. They practice "walk around" management looking for the small things people are doing well and saying "thank you." I have found it absolutely amazing the extra effort and energy that comes from an employee with a "thank you." Value added leaders give away the credit for a job well done even if they participated in getting the job done well. Value added leaders celebrate successes through award ceremonies, lunches, dinners, informal events, etc. Group recognition and appreciation events can be incredibly valuable in bonding a team when every member of the team can get together and celebrate a collective success. Value added leaders find every opportunity to "publicly" recognize people for successes.

Value added leaders let the people in the organization know they need them for the business to be successful. They let them know they can't do it alone. Value added leaders find ways to help people grow in their skills and abilities. On a regular basis, they evaluate the skills and abilities of their people, then structure a development plan specific to that individual. Bottom line: value added leadership is about influencing people not manipulating people. When value added leaders recognize and inspire people, these people are then open to being influenced by the leader's ideas, suggested ways to get better at their job, change within the business and, in nearly all cases, employees will go the extra mile for the business. Value added leaders are consistently moving people to what they are capable of becoming as human beings and employees of the business. Value added leaders truly enjoy watching people grow.

Value added leaders are authentic. They walk the talk, demonstrate what they say, manifest their words, you get what you see, are an open book, in other words, they don't try to be or do something they are not. In order to do this, value added leaders have to be well grounded in who they are and have the self-confidence and self-esteem to let the world see who they are. Don't confuse this with ego. Value added leaders are humble and content with who they are. They recognize that they are vulnerable to disappointments and mistakes, but are secure in admitting these and moving on. They don't wear a suit of armor pretending to be invincible because they know they are vulnerable. They show emotions of joy, sadness, and distress. They demonstrate they are as human as every person in the business. This creates enormous respect from employees in the organization, which in turn opens the door for the value added leaders to influence people in the organization.

Value added leader's value people. They know that, in order to add value to people, they must first value people and their individuality. One of the ways they do this is to show a sincere interest in the person. Value added leaders demonstrate human understanding. They ask questions, and then they listen. They ask about dreams, family, hobbies, passions, etc. In essence, they search for the person's story to find out what makes them tick. Value added leaders know how to get into the mind and heart of a person. Again, they ask questions and then listen very carefully for what is important to that person. Value added leaders know that, in order for them to get the performance they want, they must first know what is important to the person and then move toward finding the win-win solution. Creating a win-lose situation is not in the vocabulary of the value added leader. They know that every person is uniquely built with skills, abilities, heart, personality, and values. Unless they tap into those aspects of a person, they will not be able to create a work environment that will create a win-win for the business and the employee.

The value added leader is the visionary painter of ideas. Just as the valued added leader breathes life into the passionate objective he/she needs to be able to look into the future, with regard to that passionate objective, and then paint a picture for the organization of the ideas that will make the passionate objective a reality. It is not enough for the leaders in the organization to have ideas because, unless they can get the people in the organization to visualize and internalize those ideas, they are worthless. Those who will need to implement and execute the visionary's ideas must be able to effectively grasp those ideas and the benefit to them and the business. This then becomes the catalyst for change in the organization.

The value added leader creates and nourishes the business environment. This is an extension of the discussion on the impact of environment on brand and a well-respected image. The value added leader "demonstrates" the desired behavior of the people in the organization. Behavior, such as respect for fellow workers, decision making with integrity, trust among employees, open communication, responsibility and accountability, positive attitude, fun, valuing clients, respecting alliances, recognition for good work, receptivity to new ideas, and others. Whatever the leaders in the organization demonstrate is what will be reflected by the people in the business.

The value added leader focuses "on" the business not "in" the business. Because the value added leader is the visionary and catalyst for change, their thinking has to be macro, not micro. Yes, they do continually measure, track, and assess the detail of the business, but their thinking has to be "big picture" thinking. They cannot be the maker of the widgets on a daily basis. According to the book "E-Myth", the typical business owner is 10% entrepreneur, 20% manager, and 70% technician! I would suggest the value added leader is 70% entrepreneur, 30% manager, and 0% technician.

Up to now, I have not talked about business plans. The best business plan is a "roadmap." This plan says I want to get from here to there and, based on what I know today, this is the roadmap of how I am going to get from here to there. However, once I get started on the trip I may run into road detours, bad weather, and/or mechanical problems, which is certainly going to change my original plan and timetable for getting there. So what do I do? I stay focused on where I want to arrive, but I change my plan according to the circumstances along the way. This is what the value added leader does. He/she focuses on where the business is going and then adjusts the plan or roadmap based on what is happening in the business and the changes in the world outside the business. Changes in personnel, national, state and local economic changes, market changes, product manufacturing changes, cost changes, revenue changes, etc. The value added leader stays focused on the destination, regularly checks the roadmap, and then makes changes, if necessary, to reach the destination. Value added leaders know the importance of ensuring that the world outside is not changing faster than their business is changing on the inside.

People

The people in a healthy business vary according to the structure of the business. These groups of people can be stockholders, private investors, individual owners, a board of directors, executives, managers, skilled workers, etc. In a healthy business, the glue that binds these groups together is effective communication. In the absence of open, honest communication it is virtually impossible for these groups to work together for the benefit of the business. This is the first lesson in getting the right people in the right place. Whatever the organizational structure, healthy businesses have effective systems of communication among these groups. They don't assume communication; they have a process of communication to ensure information, both good and bad, is communicated to these groups. A healthy business does not communicate what they think a group may want to hear, but communicates accurate and real information that allows groups of people to make good decisions for the benefit of the business. A healthy business leverages the intellectual capital of these groups for the benefit of the business.

The principle tools of a healthy business are not machinery and equipment. Neither is it solely the brainpower of owners, executives, and managers. Rather the tools of a healthy business are the ideas, skills, and talents of everyone in the organization. The business world of today has moved beyond the industrial age where machinery and equipment were the driving force behind production. In today's business world it is the intellectual capital of everyone in the organization. Healthy businesses don't let anyone in the organization park their brains at the door when they arrive for work. Rather they get the right people in the right places within the organization, and then they ask questions and listen to the ideas of those people. This applies to every person from the top down.

The first step in getting the right people in the right place is to determine the human capital needs of the business. It is not finding places for people, but rather determining the needs of the business and then finding the right people to fill those needs. Depending on the nature of the business, this may be the need for people who are good at building things, good salespeople, good administrators, good at marketing, good at designing things, etc. Determine the needs of the business, define the roles, and then find the right people. So who are the right people?? They are the people that love to do the things the business needs. I cannot overemphasize they must love to do what the business needs. Study after study has shown that people who do what they love have a positive self-perception, have purpose in their work, have confidence in their work, have purpose in their work, and are very dependable because they enjoy their work, take pride in their work, strive to do their best, are enthusiastic about their work, take responsibility for their performance, and have a positive attitude, which leads us to the next aspect of getting the right people in the right place.

Getting the right people in the right place is, first, evaluation of their skills and who they are as an individual. Skills can be learned, but changing the inherent makeup of the individual is difficult for any organization. People are born with characteristics of their parents, are shaped by the beliefs and values of their parents in the early stages of their lives, are influenced by the opinions of others, are influenced by their peers, and are shaped by life experiences, good and bad. All of these factors shape the heart and spirit of the individual. They drive their values, attitudes toward others, achievement drive, and personality. In the work place, these characteristics will affect their attitude toward work and other people. Is it negative or is it positive? Are they introverted or do they thrive in a team environment? This is important based on the work the organization wants them to do. Do they view their work as a job or is it a career? Are they trustworthy? What is their attitude toward authority? Do they fight it or are they cooperative? These are only a few examples of the impact a person's "shape" has on their role in the organization. I am not suggesting this is an easy selection process. However, my experience has been that it is much better to invest in hiring the right person than to correct a hiring mistake. Getting the right people in the right place in the organization is very important.

It can be difficult to attract the right people, even after they have been identified as the right person for the right place in the organization. The most critical factor is the environment. Studies have shown that money is typically not the primary reason quality people choose to associate with an organization. In most cases, it is not the opportunity to climb the corporate ladder. There are more important factors for these people which, for the most part, encompasses environment.

One of the factors is the opportunity to grow personally. Good people don't like to be put in a position where their personal growth is limited. As we discussed earlier these are people who have high self-esteem, are confident, strive to do their best, challenge themselves to do even better, have purpose in their work, and get fulfillment from their work. To limit their growth will limit them, which, in turn, will limit the full value the organization can receive from these people. Therefore, the environment encourages and nurtures their growth. Healthy businesses give them space to grow. Not physical space, but the space to be innovative in their work. Healthy businesses encourage them to take calculated risks and, if they make a mistake, to learn from those mistakes. The business supports training to increase skill levels. The combination of encouragement, training, support, and the space to grow will attract the right people.

Once the right people are identified, and hired, how does a healthy business keep these people? In addition to the proper environment, reward and recognition are critically important. One aspect of reward is monetary. My experience has been that it can be very difficult to structure a monetary reward system that works for both the people and the business. A healthy business links the monetary reward system to the "passionate objective" with written and very clearly measurable benchmarks. This system basically says that, if the business is not on target with regard to the passionate objective, the right people are not performing at a level to be rewarded. I have been involved in creating these programs' and they can be demanding to create. However, if they are clear, simple to understand, and linked to the passionate objective, they are incredibly powerful.

Healthy businesses create, support, and promote "self-leadership" among their people. One of the aspects of "self-leadership" is self-confidence. There has been widespread debate whether self-confidence is in a person's DNA or whether it can be developed. I fall in the camp that it can be developed if the culture supports the tools to develop self-confidence. Self-confidence can't be developed if the culture does not create opportunities for people to have successes and failures. People must be given the opportunity to make decisions and choices that have an uncertain outcome. If the outcome is a success, then the organization can recognize, reward, and celebrate the success. If the outcome is a mistake, now the organization has the opportunity to help the employee evaluate the "why" of the mistake, evaluate how the mistake can be avoided in the future, and then "encourage" the person. Encouragement meaning that they need to know the mistake is not about them as a person , but rather it is the decision and let them know they need to continue taking risks in the future. What will happen? Eventually they will learn from these mistakes, they will make fewer mistakes in the future, and their self-confidence will grow accordingly.

"Self-leadership" is having a healthy perspective on who they are as a unique human being and liking the person they have become. Self-love is critical to self-leadership. People can't add value to a business until they are secure in who they are. If they are secure in themselves, they have a positive attitude toward events and people, they are optimistic about goals and possibilities, they are fun to be around, they are sincerely interested in others and their welfare because they are secure in their own welfare, they are healthy because they like themselves and like taking care of themselves, they look good because they like themselves and they like to look good, they welcome honest feedback in how they can improve their performance, they take initiative, they are energetic and enthusiastic.

Finally, self-leadership is about achievement. People who are well grounded in self-leadership only need to know how to win the game and they will find the ways to win. Yes, they need coaching, but the drive to win is deeply ingrained into who they are and they 'self motivate' themselves. These are the thoroughbreds of the organization. Once they are out of the gate, they don't need spurring or a whip, all they need is someone to keep them going down the track and guiding them toward the finish line. They will charge to the finish based on their need and desire to achieve all they can achieve.

The Product

In our discussion of brand and image, we talked about there being many aspects regarding whether brand and image are positive or negative. One of those aspects is to have a quality product. It is virtually impossible to have a positive brand and image without a quality product that the market desires, wants or needs. A product being defined as a tangible product, such as consumer goods or an intangible product being a service provided to clients.

However, it is not enough to have a quality product; a healthy business must have a quality product that the market desires, wants or needs. One of the early lessons I learned in starting businesses is that, no matter how excited I am about my product, if the marketplace is not excited about the product fulfilling their real or perceived need, desire, or want, the business will struggle, if not fail. If the marketplace does not need, desire, or want the product, then the business must create in the minds and heart of the prospective client the need, desire, and/or want for the product. This often times is a slow, frustrating, and expensive approach. It may require a considerable amount of time through advertising and other means of exposure to get the marketplace to buy the product. This approach I describe as a "marketing driven approach." It means that a considerable amount of marketing will be needed to establish acceptance in the marketplace.

In late 1980 I co-founded an "employee leasing" business. Today they are known as "professional employer organizations". When we first learned of the employee leasing concept we were convinced that there was a tremendous market for such services. Why wouldn't small businesses that could not afford their own human resources department want to pay a reasonable fee to outsource those needs to an employee leasing firm? The concept was that the employees of the business would contractually be employees of the employee leasing firm and they would be "leased" to the business. Therefore, the business didn't have to commit resources to payroll, state and federal filings, hiring, terminations, employee manuals, etc. They could then direct all of their resources toward the manufacture of their products and/or services - A great deal for the small business, right?

As we approached businesses with our services, we met a cool reception. The business owners had no objections to our fee structure and the quality of services. However, they had a real problem with "letting go" of their employees. In their mind, if they leased the employees from our firm they felt they "lost control" and that didn't feel good to them. Our challenge then became convincing them that they still controlled all of the employee's activity; we simply handled all of the human resources functions. Because we had not adequately tested our market as to whether they felt a need, desire or want for our services we invested a tremendous amount of financial resources marketing to our potential market. Thus, we took the "marketing driven" approach which can be very costly for a business.

A more effective and cost efficient approach is the "market driven" approach. With this approach, the marketplace has already identified a real or perceived need, desire, or want for the product. This is the leverage of research prior to investing in the structure of a business around a product concept. If you already have a business, which is struggling in selling enough product, then I suggest you analyze why you are not selling enough product. First, ask the market through a variety of survey tools what they like, and don't like, about your product. Second, test other markets. It may very well be that, what you think is your market, is in fact not the marketplace that needs, desires, or wants the product. There are a variety of research tools available that will allow you to "test the waters," so to speak, in other markets.

Effective and Efficient Processes

The term "processes" is synonymous with systems in this discussion. It is any sequence of events that creates more efficiency and effectiveness in the operation of the business. I am not going to talk about technology as a process because I believe technology is a "tool" that can be used in many of these processes to improve efficiencies and effectiveness. Regardless of whether a business's product is tangible or intangible, each of these processes is encompassed in every business. The processes are: product manufacturing, product distribution, client service, compliance, and money management.

First, let's talk about product manufacturing. It is impossible to have efficiency and effectiveness in product manufacturing without trustworthy alliances with the suppliers of the product's components. Again, this is true in tangible and intangible product businesses. In a tangible business it is the nuts and bolts components, and in the intangible business, it is the suppliers of information or the suppliers of the tools necessary to perform the service. In the financial services business it is suppliers of information, and in a commercial cleaning business, it is the supplier of the tools and cleaners necessary to provide their cleaning service. In any case, every business needs a trustworthy alliance with their supplier. Remember, if the supplier cannot or will not supply the business with the component parts, the business cannot manufacture their product. It is just that simple.

Healthy businesses know that the first step in a trustworthy alliance is to treat the supplier as they would want to be treated. One aspect of this is to have a process in place to plan when the components will be needed for the manufacture of the product so the business does not have to "demand" delivery of a component which the supplier may not be in a position to deliver. A second aspect is to pay the supplier for the component per the terms of the agreement. Unless it is a part of the agreement for a specific delayed payment period, it is not the supplier's responsibility to finance the component for the business. The business expects to be paid per the terms of their agreement with a buyer of their product. Therefore, the business should pay the supplier per the terms of their agreement as the buyer of the supplier's product. A business cannot have an efficient and effective process of product manufacturing it they do not have the components to manufacture their product. The supplier is in 100% control of whether the business gets the component in a timely manner for the manufacture of the product, or if the business receives the component at all. Therefore, trustworthy alliances with suppliers is critical for an efficient and effective process of product manufacturing.

A second aspect of effective and efficient product manufacturing is the process of making the product. For example, accounting firms have a process of sending out forms for their clients to pre-fill containing the information necessary to complete a tax return. The next step is the meeting to discuss the information. The accounting firm then prepares the tax return. The client then reviews the information and the accounting firm completes the return, the client signs and then sends the form to the IRS.

Today many of the steps in this process are done electronically, leveraging the tool of technology. If the business manufactures cars, the process probably involves processes consisting of human functions, robotic functions, mechanical functions, etc. Regardless of the product being manufactured, it is critical to maximize efficiency and effectiveness in the manufacture of the product. Healthy businesses regularly evaluate their product manufacturing process. It may be that there has been a new technology developed that is more efficient than what they are using today. As you might expect, effective and efficient product manufacturing can be a major factor in whether a business is profitable. It may also mean the business can be more competitive in their marketplace because they can more competitively price their product with an efficient product manufacturing process.

A second process is product distribution. In this discussion, I am encompassing the marketing, sale, and delivery of the product. Before any of these can be designed, the business must first decide on the method of distribution. Will the business distribute the product "in-house," outsource distribution or a combination of both? When I was associated with a Fortune 500 company in the financial services industry, the decision was made to take the combination approach. We had a group of producers who were "captive" in the sense that their contract with the company stated that their primary responsibility was to promote and sell the company's products.

A second distribution arm was "independent" distribution meaning these producers had a contract with the company stating they would put the company's products on their "product shelf." If they found the right situation to promote the product, and they made the decision to use the product, then they had access to the product and the right to use that product. The combination approach can present challenges with regard to marketing materials, market positioning, potential market conflict, etc. However, it does create a broader penetration of the marketplace while "averaging" the high cost of "in-house" distribution with the lower cost of "outsourced" distribution. The point is that the business must first decide on the method of distribution.

The first step in marketing is to determine who the market is for the business's product. This can vary over time depending on changes in the product and changes in the desires, wants and needs of the marketplace. As we discussed earlier, healthy businesses know that first determining "if" there is a market that has a want, desire and/or need for the product, is best before actually creating a business structure and beginning the manufacture of the product. Once the market is determined, the next question is whether the product is a "commodity" product or a "relationship" product. The marketing approach will vary for each product. The marketing approach for a consumer product like beverages (a commodity product) is quite different than marketing for a financial plan (a relationship product). A business can market a beverage via the internet, vending machines, retail outlets, etc., because people simply need access to the consumer product and a convenient way to purchase the product. However, a person wanting to plan for their financial future is not going to purchase a financial plan without first establishing a relationship with someone they trust with their personal information and confident they will receive a complete and objective plan for their financial future. A business can market the beverage without a relationship; they just need a quality product and provide access to the product. A financial planning business must have a marketing plan that, first and foremost, creates an opportunity to begin building a relationship.

Depending on whether the product is a "commodity" or "relationship" product, the next step is to decide on the "method" of marketing. Considerations should include print advertising, internet, websites, television, radio, networking, seminars, referral marketing, billboards, and others. Obviously, budget considerations come into play in this decision, but the point is that there are a number of ways to market products. Healthy businesses know the importance of finding the approach, or combination of approaches, which are going to be most efficient and effective. Not only is the method important but the message is equally important. Is it a message of competitive price, product differentiation, product innovation, and value added that will make someone's life easier, more comfortable, more fun, and more fulfilling? Maybe it is a message of appealing to ego or fear. Remember, businesses only exist if the marketplace wants the business to exist. If the marketplace does not want, desire, or need the product, the business will not survive. In an earlier discussion, I said the marketplace may already know that they want, desire, or need a product, or a business may have to mentally and/or emotionally move the marketplace to want, desire, or need the product. My point is that healthy businesses know that an effective and financially efficient method of marketing, along with a message that will "move" the marketplace to purchase their product, are critical to the success of the business.

Now let's talk about the sales process. Many times businesses confuse marketing and sales as being a combined process. Both are essential, but they are distinctly different processes. The marketing process gets the attention of the client or prospective client. The sales process is what happens once the business has captured the attention of the client or prospective client. Any good sales process focuses on demonstrating the benefits of the product for the buyer. Too many times the sales process is focused on the features of the product from the businesses point of view. The prospective buyer only wants to know about features as they relate to their benefit. A good sales process is always focused on the client and should never address the benefits to the salesperson and/or the business. The prospective client only wants to know how the products are going to meet their want, desire, and/or need. A good sales process should be simple to understand and complete. Sometimes sales people, even successful sales people, get carried away in talking about how much they know about the product. All the prospective client really cares about is how much the salesperson cares about them and meeting their want, desire, or need. The prospective client assumes they know a great deal about the product. Even if a human being is not involved in the sale, as in the case of most consumer goods, the process of buying should be simple.

I once owned a gourmet coffee business. My business distributed a wide variety of gourmet coffees within businesses via a vending device. I quickly learned that the client did not want to deal with any form of currency, either coins or bills when they wanted a cup of gourmet coffee. They preferred a simple token or prepaying with a debit card that could be used via a scanner on the machine. Healthy businesses know that in the sales process the prospective client is the focus of everything communicated and the process of buying the product must be as simple as possible.

The third step in product distribution is product delivery. Too many times businesses and salespeople get wrapped up in the selling process and then lose interest in getting the product delivered in a timely fashion. I believe ineffective delivery of a product is one of the reasons buyers have a negative perception of salespeople. When the product is not delivered when promised the client perceives that the salesperson and business does not care about them and all they care about is getting paid for the sale. How do you feel if you take your car to be serviced or repaired and it takes longer than you were promised? It creates a negative attitude, right? It's because you expect the business to deliver as promised. Remember our earlier discussion about needing seven positive comments to neutralize one negative comment? When a business does not deliver their product or service when they commit to deliver, many times it creates a negative attitude that in turn will impact future decisions to buy a product from the business, and if communicated to others in the marketplace, may impact the opportunity for future sales. Healthy businesses know the distribution process must be complete—from marketing to sales to timely and effective delivery of the product.

The effective and efficient process following delivery is client service. There are two aspects to client service. One is "reactive service" and the second is "proactive service." Reactive service is responding to the requests of the client with regard to the use or performance of the product. In the insurance business this may be changing beneficiaries on a policy or changing the mode of premium payments. Healthy businesses recognize the importance of responding to these requests with empathy "we are sorry that happened" or "we will be happy to help you with your request." The message they send is that we value you as a client and we will do everything we can to help you with your request. Now I recognize that every business has clients with unreasonable requests sometimes, which will require diplomacy and patience. It may very well be that a decision needs to be made if the business even wants the client. Healthy businesses consistently evaluate the human and financial cost of keeping unreasonable clients. They choose who they want to be their clients.

After responding with empathy to a service request, the next step is to fulfill the request in a timely manner. Just as in the delivery process of distribution, by not responding in a timely manner the message sent by the business is that the client's request is not important. Reality is that in reactive service the request may not be able to be fulfilled within the period of time promised. That is okay, but what is not okay, is to fail to communicate with the client that more time will be required. People understand that things happen but, when that message is not communicated, it sends the message that the business does not care about them. What goes through the client's mind is that other clients are more important than them. Common sense in human relations is the guiding principle of "reactive service, " and healthy businesses ensure it is permeated throughout their service process.

The second aspect of client service is "proactive service." "Proactive service" is the intentional reaching out to clients. The primary goal of "proactive service" is building a stronger relationship with the client. It can be very expensive to find and secure a client during the marketing process. Therefore, healthy businesses have a proactive service component in their business to build on the relationship with the client. One way is to communicate to the client that the business values them as a client. This could be a regular "thank you" for choosing the product. It could be appreciation events. The important thing is communication. Whether it is written, verbal, or face to face the client needs to know the business did not just want to sell them a product, but rather they want to build a relationship with them.

Another component in "proactive service" is to ask the client what they want, desire, or need from the product. This can be valuable insight in the development of new products or how to make the product even better for them or future clients. Two things are accomplished in this form of proactive service. First, the client feels important because you demonstrate you value their opinion. Second, the business gains insight into their marketplace and how they can more effectively and efficiently manufacture a product the marketplace wants, desires, or needs and the business may gain insight with regard to how they can more efficiently and effectively distribute their product.

Another component of effective and efficient processes is compliance. In my business career, I have been involved in insurance and securities related financial services companies. In highly regulated industries such as these, it is imperative to have effective and efficient processes for complying with local, state, and national regulatory bodies. In recent years the importance of compliance supervision has escalated dramatically. Today, in these industries, virtually all correspondence sent and received by personnel in these offices, especially correspondence to and from clients, must be reviewed and signed by a compliance officer of the company or an approved principal of the firm. This is also true with regard to marketing materials used with the public and other forms of advertising. Failure to have effective and efficient processes for complying with these requirements could have very negative consequences for a company, potentially resulting in individual or class action lawsuits.

However, it is not only in highly regulated industries that there is a need for effective and efficient compliance processes, it is imperative in every business within every industry because there are compliance elements inherent in every business. Every business is expected to comply with payroll filing requirements, hiring guidelines, termination guidelines, safety procedures, and others depending on the type of business being conducted. Every business must review and examine the compliance regulations specific to their business and ensure that effective and efficient processes are in place to ensure compliance with those regulations. Fines, lawsuits, suspension of business activities, and other negative consequences could result if these processes are not in place.

The final process to be discussed is money management. I am sure this sounds like a logical and common sense thing for every business to do, but in many cases, it is not given the process attention it deserves. I am going to talk about the flow of money in and out of a business shortly, but first I want to address the management process of money in a business.

Creating an effective and efficient process of money management in a business is first to determine "who" in the business is involved in the flow of money. Who receives money and who manages money in the business? In a vending business, most likely the person servicing the vending machine collects the money, it is delivered back to someone at the business office, that person or someone else puts the money somewhere in a safe, the bank, or some other location, then someone uses that money to pay bills, payroll, etc. In other words, all money in a business has a "flow, " and it is important to decide what that flow is going to be, and then decide who in the organization is going to be involved in that flow. Obviously, there is going to be someone, a manager, owner, bookkeeper, someone who is going to decide where, when, and how the money flows out of the business, but one or more people in the business may be involved in the actual flow and management of money inside the business. Therefore, effective and efficient processes need to be in place to monitor the flow of money through each stage of money flowing into the business and as it flows out of the business. In the absence of this effective and efficient process, there is room for substantial error, loss of money, potential fraud, inaccurate financial records, and other negative consequences for the business.

Risk Management

The first step in risk management is to identify controllable risks, and those that are outside the control of the business, or uncontrollable risks. In most cases, uncontrollable risks are national, state, and local economic changes. Economic changes, such as inflation, unemployment changes, interest rates, and others. For the most part, legislative law changes are uncontrollable. True, lobbying efforts by industry associations can impact legislative decisions which warrant involvement in these associations, but for one or a few businesses to focus human and financial resources on such issues will have little impact on these decisions, which means these are uncontrollable. A natural disaster's impact on a business is logically not controllable. The point is to evaluate in the business the risks that are controllable and those that are not controllable. It is a waste of energy and resources for a business to try and control uncontrollable risks. So what are controllable risks in a business: managing the risk of losing assets, both tangible and intangible, business conduct, business succession, and loss of key employees are some common risk management areas in a business.

Managing the risk of losing assets. Assets can be lost in a number of ways such as natural disasters, fire, theft, and accidents. Obviously, first and foremost, these risks are managed through the transfer of risk to insurance companies. However, there are additional ways to manage these risks. For example, potential fires can be avoided by keeping flammable products from potential ignition sources and stored properly. Theft can be avoided by having procedures in place to accurately supervise and account for the flow of money, products, raw materials, client information, business records, equipment, and other assets of the business. Often times businesses get so involved in the manufacture of their products they lose sight of the need to manage the risk until a major loss has occurred. Accidents can be avoided through proper training and evaluating the processes in the business to identify potential areas of accidents and then modifying or eliminating those processes to avoid accidents.

This applies to tangible as well as intangible product businesses. Manufacturers of tangible products, like cars and equipment, and intangible products, like paperwork for clients' investments, insurance policies, tax returns, etc. All of these are potential areas accidents in a business can occur. Effective management of these risks can prevent shutdowns of production, lawsuits, and other consequences that could result in the loss of financial assets. Most importantly, managing the risk of accidents can avoid the loss of the business's most important asset - their employees.

Another area of controllable risk management is in business conduct. Four subjects I want to address in this area are: (1) damage caused by faulty product, (2) improper distribution of a product, (3) ethical business practices, and (4) financial reporting. First, let's talk about damage caused by faulty product. I am sure the first thing that comes to mind in this area is the recall of automobiles. My guess is that many of you have been notified that your automobile needed to be taken into the dealership to have a faulty system or part repaired and/or replaced. This has multiple negative implications for the business. First is the negative message to the market place that the product is inferior and is subject to repair. This is a best case scenario for the automobile manufacturer because it has not resulted in accidents or deaths. I am sure you can recall cars and SUV's in the past that, unfortunately, have had this experience. In any case, this scenario could have a negative impact on future sales and client loyalty. Another negative implication is the additional cost to the automobile manufacturer of parts and labor to make the necessary repairs. This obviously can have a negative impact on the profitability of the business. Again, this can also have a negative impact on intangible product businesses, such as preparers of tax returns, insurance policies, investment products, etc.

A second area is business conduct risk management in product distribution. The biggest factor here is the method through which the product is distributed. If mechanically distributed, such as a vending machine, then the safety of the client in receiving the product is important. If distributed via mail, then ensuring the product is packaged and arrives safely is important. If through human distribution, then how the transaction is handled is paramount. What the salesperson says is very important. In heavily regulated industries, such as financial services, what is said and how the product is represented is very important, as well as to whom they are promoting the product. For example, certain investment products are not suited for everyone. These products should match the risk tolerance and objectives of the client or prospective client. In less regulated industries, the product should be represented as to the capabilities of its performance and not over represented to the buying public. An over representation of the capabilities of the product could lead to accusations of false advertising, or other negative consequences, potentially leading to lawsuits. The best rule of thumb is to accurately represent the performance of the product or even slightly under represent the performance, so the experience the customer has with the product exceeds the expectation that has been implanted in their mind. It is always better to have their expectations exceeded versus not met.

A third area is ethical business practices. Ethical can have many definitions depending on the business. In the manufacturing world, it is building the best product possible at a cost that will give the business some level of profitability. In the services sector, it is delivering the best service possible for a reasonable cost. The best rule of thumb in ethical business practices is "intent." If decisions are made with the intent of deceiving, cheating, lying to, and/or defrauding employees, clients, suppliers, financiers, alliances, authorities, and/or the public, then they have acted with the intent to conduct unethical practices. However, if the intent is to be honest, caring, focused on quality, service oriented, fulfilling commitments, and taking responsibility, then the business is taking an ethical approach to business conduct. Obviously, there are many negative consequences for a business that is caught taking an unethical approach to business conduct, not the least of which may be lawsuits, loss of business, criminal actions, loss of relationships, and potential shutdown of the business. Therefore, no matter how dire the situation may be, whether it be low sales volume, increasing costs, production problems, etc., it will always be in the best long-term interests of the business to take the high road and conduct the business in an ethical manner.

Finally, I want to talk about financial reporting as it relates to business conduct. In the area of financial management, accurate and timely reporting is very important. This could be reporting to financing entities such as banks, investors, or governmental entities. How many times have you heard of businesses getting into serious trouble because they did not provide accurate and timely financial information to the government? This is not limited to the IRS; it also encompasses payroll reporting and other financial reports per regulatory requirements. Relationships with banks and investors can be negatively impacted if they receive inaccurate financial information in making decisions relative to the business and, if not delivered in a timely manner, it sends a message that the business does not value the relationship with them.

The first step in accurate reporting is to have accurate financial records. This means the person or persons responsible for financial management need to have access to all of the relevant financial business information. This includes sales, cost of goods, payroll, benefits costs, financing costs, if applicable, revenue from sources other than sales, depreciation, and other financial information in the business to ensure they can compile a complete and accurate financial report. The second step is to have a system in place of reporting to ensure the financial reports are delivered in a timely manner. This will vary among businesses, and the nature of their business, but some system of reporting must be in place.

The next area of risk management is business succession. In other words, managing the risk of the business continuing to survive, grow, and/or prosper as a result of an event, such as the death or disability of the business owner/CEO, a retirement, or decision to become inactive in the business. This is a very real issue today given the number of businesses with owners 50 years old and older. Many of those businesses have no written plan in place, given one of the above events occurs, and those that do have written plans often times do not have an accompanying funding vehicle to execute the plan. So many times business owners and CEOs get caught up in the hectic pace of working "in" the business and don't allow time to work "on" the business such as getting critical plans, like business succession plans, in place. The risk is the business does not grow, prosper and, in the extreme case, survive.

The first step in creating a good plan to manage these risks is to determine who is going to step into the business owner's or CEO's shoes when they die, become disabled, retire, or step away from the business. It could be a key employee, a family member, an interested investor, or other party, that the business decides, in advance, is willing and capable of ensuring the continued success of the business. Once that is determined, then a written plan of "how" the transaction is going to take place must be created. Finally, any funding vehicles necessary to execute the transition must be put in place to fund the written plan once the event occurs. These funding vehicles can take many forms, such as life insurance proceeds, disability insurance proceeds, bank loans, a separate account funded over time to accumulate funds, and others. The important thing is to have the funds available per the written agreement when the event occurs.

In the event of retirement, one of the critical issues is how the business owner funds their retirement living costs, without continuing to draw money from the business when they are no longer active in the business. If the business owner continues to take money out of the business for retirement living costs, at the same time the business is paying someone to replace the owner in his/her duties, will the business have enough cash flow to continue to grow, prosper, and/or survive?

A final area of risk management is the loss of one or more key employees. The term "key employee" is just what it implies. It is the loss of one or more people in the business that are "key" to the business continuing to grow and prosper. These are people who have roles and responsibilities that are the life blood of the business. In the event one or more of these people become disabled, die, retire, or decide to leave the business, it will constrict the flow of life giving blood to the business, causing the business to suffer. The risks of disability and death are relatively easy to manage by transferring the risk to insurance companies. The retirement risk can be managed by having a plan in place to replace the key executive. This can be accomplished by identifying that person, far in advance, of the retirement of the key executive. The next step is to implement a plan to train the person identified for the skill necessary to fulfill those roles and responsibilities and then give them the opportunities to participate in those roles and responsibilities. This is important so they can make mistakes while the key executive is still active in the business so the key executive can mentor them and help them learn from those mistakes. As they make fewer mistakes, they will develop the self-confidence and skills necessary to effectively fill the shoes of the key executive when they retire.

The issue of the key executive making the conscious choice to leave the business is not as easy to manage, but it requires a combination of many things to manage this risk effectively. It is a combination of sincerely, and consistently, communicating to them their value to the business and then having a plan in place that rewards them for their contribution to the business.

The first of these, communicating their value to the business, entails words of appreciation, opportunities for them to develop personally, public and private recognition for good work, and creating opportunities for them to stretch beyond their capabilities of today to become even more valuable to the business. In today's business world it is almost a given that employees receive a minimum of health and retirement benefits through the business. For key employees, adding enhanced life and disability insurance for them and their family, or other forms of benefits that are important to them, is important in keeping these key employees. In most cases, the financial plan is the most important element in managing the risk of losing key employees. There are many different forms these plans can take and will vary according to the nature of the business and the financial ability of the business to fund these plans. The most effective are those linked to performance. This is good for the business and good for the key employee. In designing these plans, the first step is to match the plan with the goals of the business. If the goal is growth, then the key executive compensation plan should be designed around growth. If the primary goal is profitability, then the key executive compensation plan should be designed around profitability of the business. These may vary over time-based on the development stages of the business and the executive. The important thing is for the business to determine the vision of where the business wants to get to, and then financially rewarding key employees as benchmarks are achieved in making that vision a reality. This is a win-win for the business and the key employee and is very powerful in managing the risk of losing one or more key employees.

Money "In" and Money "Out"

This is really a very simple concept, but not necessarily an easy concept, for businesses to put into practice. To begin the discussion, I want to explore the various sources of money into a business which, by no means, is necessarily a comprehensive list. Of course, money can flow into a business from institutions. This could be money from banks, savings and loans, government programs, and other lending institutions. This money typically flows into the business via loans with a promise to pay this money back to the financial institution with interest. Money can flow via personal savings accounts or other forms of accounts where money has been accumulated for the purpose of having it flow into the business. Money can flow via investment vehicles such as investment funds, individual stock purchases, private equity, bonds, etc., which receive a fixed, variable, or combination of both for a return on their investment. And money can flow into a business via the money received from the sale of the business's products and services. Money can also flow into a business via the returns it receives on investments the business has made.

Money flows out of a business in a variety of ways as well. It flows out in the form of compensation to employees, to help create more "in flow" of money into the business such as branding, image building, marketing, and other forms to generate revenue from the sale of the business's products and services. Money flows out to providers of services such as accounting, equipment maintenance, and other services required by the business. Money flows out of the business to purchase the components necessary to manufacture products and services. Money flows out of the business for customer service. Money flows out to manage the risks inherent in the business. Money also flows out of the business to pay for the cost of money flowing into the business, which leads me to the discussion of "more of the right money in than money out."

It is understandable that in a startup business or a business in the early stages of development there is a need to pay for money to flow into the business from lending institutions and investment vehicles. And certainly, for more mature businesses who want to grow and expand, there may be a need for this type of money flow into the business. However, this flow of money into the business comes with a cost, and that cost is typically fixed, variable or a combination of both. Obviously the more costs in a business, the greater challenge in achieving profitability for the business. Profitability is a major component for the business to grow, prosper and/or survive. My point in this discussion is that healthy businesses regularly evaluate the flow of money into the business and the impact that flow is having on profitability. Depending on interest rates and/or the expected percentage return on investment lending institutions and/or investment vehicles may be the 'right' money into the business. This is obviously true in low-interest rate environments. However, I would suggest that in most cases the best form of 'right' money into the business is through the sale of the businesses products and services and further, the quicker a business can get into the financial position to be self-supporting and begin to build cash reserves for future growth, expansion and/or survival the more control the business will have over their ultimate destiny. It is imperative businesses regularly evaluate this flow of money into the business, the impact that flow is having on the cost of their products, the impact on their sales volume and the impact on their profitability.

Nurture the Plant

To complete the portrait of a healthy business, I want to talk about nurturing the plant. In my youth, I lived in a small farming community. It was a great life. My favorite time of the year was in the spring. The trees came to life and began to grow leaves, the flowers began to bloom, and we went to the fields to plant the season's crops. We prepared the soil to receive the seed, then we were very careful to plant the seed at the proper depth, because if we planted it too shallow, it would not get enough nutrients and moisture to sprout and, if we planted the seed too deep it would lay dormant lacking the proper conditions to sprout. Once the seed began to sprout and grow, the real work began, and that was nurturing the plant. We had to ensure we gave the plant the attention it needed to grow and ultimately produce. Each year was always different in nurturing the plant. Some years we needed to give it more food, in the form of fertilizers, some years weeds wanted the space occupied by the plant and, therefore, we had to remove the weeds, so the plant had enough space to root and grow, and some years the ground would get hard, for lack of rain, and we would have to till the soil around the plant to ensure the plant had enough air to survive. Every year we had to evaluate the conditions and decide what we needed to do to nurture the plant so it would grow and produce.

A healthy business is just like that plant. Once you have planted the seed and implemented the things we have talked about today to grow a healthy business, you can't stop there. The business must be regularly evaluated as to its health, and decisions must be made to ensure it continues to grow and prosper. One of the things to evaluate is whether the business inside is growing relative to the world outside. Are the products and services the business provides, still the right products for the world outside the business? The technology sector is a good example. Think back to the first computer you bought. Mine was an Apple II. At the time that computer was awesome! But think what would have happened if Apple would have stopped evaluating changes going on in the world outside the business versus the products being created inside the business. We probably would not hear much about Apple today.

We have seen the same in the financial services industry. Banks are no longer banks; they are financial services businesses providing insurance products and investment products to their clients. Insurance companies are no longer insurance companies, they are financial service firms providing investment products and banking products. What have they done? They have changed inside the business based on changes in the world outside the business. Healthy businesses nurture the plant by evaluating the world on the outside and making decisions on how to change on the inside.

Healthy businesses nurture the plant, the business, by evaluating their people, their products and services, customer service, their marketplace, their branding, and their processes. They ask questions, they observe, they visualize, they strategize, and they analyze "what if's." What if this happens? What if that happens? In other words, they are regularly examining the plant, the business, to say based on what we know today, what do we need to do to nurture the business to ensure the growth and prosperity of the business?

The point is that it is not enough to create a business. If the business is not regularly nurtured, it will lack the nutrients it needs to grow and prosper, and it could ultimately begin to wilt and potentially die. However, if nurtured properly, it will grow and produce as long as it gets the attention it needs.

Conclusion

My hope is that I have planted one or more seeds in your minds that will sprout and grow and have a positive impact on you, your business and your family. What you do with these business insights is now up to you. My purpose is to merely share with you my thoughts relative to my observations and experiences over the past forty years in business. To share with you a model of what I believe to be a healthy business. I certainly don't profess this to be "the" model nor to suggest there are no other business models that create healthy businesses. It is my perspective and only my perspective. However, if one or more of these ideas breathes new life into your business, then it has been worthwhile for me to write this book.

Thank you for allowing me to share my experiences and observations with you!

To inquire about Business Consulting and Event Speaking Services, or to comment on this book, please contact Jerry at : AssociatesJW@yahoo.com.

www.ingramcontent.com/pod-product-compliance
Lightning Source LLC
Chambersburg PA
CBHW061220180526
45170CB00003B/1090